FINISHING LINE PRESS

www.finishinglinepress.com

Alexithymia: The Written Words

poems by

Katarina Boudreaux

Finishing Line Press
Georgetown, Kentucky

Alexithymia: The Written Words

ACKNOWLEDGMENTS

"Penny Candles" and "Amorous Intent" originally published in *Issue I,* The
Borfski Press. "In Nurseries" and "Revelation Plates" originally published by
Black Napkin Press.

Dedicated to Kuillin James; my thanks to my friends and family.

Publisher: Leah Maines

Editor: Christen Kincaid

Cover Art: Sandra P. Boudreaux

Author Photo: Maziar Amirani

Cover Design: Elizabeth Maines McCleavy

Printed in the USA on acid-free paper.
Order online: www.finishinglinepress.com
also available on amazon.com

Author inquiries and mail orders:
Finishing Line Press
P. O. Box 1626
Georgetown, Kentucky 40324
U. S. A.

Table of Contents

AMOROUS INTENT

To know love
is to feel
the absence
of it more keenly
than its presence.

To speak love—
that's the
harder thing.

EVE WAITING

We are symbiotic—
the apple within,
tree without.

How small the seed
that sprouts,
how large the reach
of the sapling.

Ten fingers...
hoping for toes.

THE FALL OF LEAVING

We stewed apples
and pretended
it was cold outside.

The rains came,
and you sat at
the wobbly end
of the glass table
drinking spiced tea
from the pottery
we fashioned
before the lights
went out.

When the moon
was no longer
with us,
I held your hand
and begged you
to open up,
but my words
fell about you
like snowflakes
in the middle
of June.

Leaves covered
you in a slow
blanket of decay
before I left.

PENNY CANDLES

She blew the
last candle out,
and for the first time
after two years
of suffering over
her beloved's death,
she did not question
how she had treated
those last days,
but instead,
considered what
she would eat
for dinner.

PEELING FRUIT

1.
The ten o'clock news
ran the story
but left out the most
important details,
like how she didn't
flinch when he finally
pulled the trigger,
and how alone he felt
until he pulled it again.

2.
Her fingers sticky
from the juice,
she turned the water
on and let it run
over the edge
of the sink like
the waterfall she
never did see after
they put her mother
in the body bag
and her father
in the back of
the police car.

3.
Everyday still
felt like the first,
though they assured
her each week
that the expectation
of something
about to happen
would lessen
with time.

In the beginning,
she felt like
her mind was
playing tricks—
the creak of
floorboard,
a door opening.

After a year
she realized
the only tricks
she had were
the ones that came
in a bottle
and made her
sleep at night.

4.
Lonely in the crowd,
she moved on,
the presence of one
a sharp reminder
of how three felt.

A stranger asked
for directions,
but she didn't answer,
as her only salvation
lay at the river.

The walk was not long,
but each step was
an eternity of
swimming through faces—
her face, theirs,
drowning for peace.

FINAL QUESTIONS

No news was
acceptable
until the final moment
when she wondered
if he'd ever seen
the ocean in CA,
or eaten something
that made him
question the rest
of his gustatory
experiences.

She wanted to know
if he had ever
laughed until
his insides hurt,
cried until there
was no moisture
left in the folds
of his skin.

She didn't know.

Then she wished
she'd at least
have called
on his birthday
one of the years
after the blow-up.

CONFESSIONAL PAPERS

The table was cold,
the lights a jellyfish
suspended.
Paper bunched
beneath my body.

Hijacked,
my spirit became
a small bird
freezing next to
the other body
deep within.

The door opened
and closed several
times, a deep
bass line
beneath the sound
of my bones
letting go of what
would not be
before my mind
shut off.

IN NURSERIES

In the half-light,
she could not tell
their faces apart.

      Hush now.

Knowing she would
not see them again,
she touched their
cheeks with her
index finger
and drew careful
heart shapes.

      The cradle rocks.

The others were coming,
and she understood
her time with them
was complete.

      Papa will buy you...

She whispered not
I love you,
but I can not love you
more than this
and walked away.

      The bough breaks.

WARM FOR APRIL

He threw a party
the night before,
loud music and
louder conversation,
his mind a wheel
rolling down.

When the car pulled
up the next morning,
her hair a shock
of yellow against
the granular silver
of the cheap paint job
he'd completed
three years ago,
he shot five times.

She fell to
the ground,
no longer capable
of leaving him.
He thought he heard
the cries of his
four and one year old,
but it was Friday,
and they were
at day care.

The ground was
already red when
he placed the metal
to his head and pulled
the trigger.

It was warm
for April.

THE HIGH DIVE

Our bodies thin,
we ran off
the high dive,
arms flailing,
mouths sucking air
as if life itself
was trying to
ride in our wake.

Your eyes were
like plates
that I wanted
to fill.

The seasons changed
and so did our outsides,
though my insides
never let go
of our hands intertwined,
weightless, magic—
the unspoken
lingering between us
as we fell.

REMEMBERED VERBIAGE

After bath time,
Mom would sit me
on the tall stool
in front of her
heart shaped mirror.

I would watch
her reflection as
she patiently combed
through my tangles,
each stroke a silent
I love you.

We were never
good at words,
and I would complain
that the comb
hurt, but I loved her
for working through
all my knots.

MINOR INCONVENIENCES

We walked to
the ocean's edge
expecting great things
of it and us.

There was a dead
horseshoe crab
and several shells
of different shapes.

I picked up
the roundest one
and put it in
my pocket as
a reminder of
the day the tent
would not be
staked.

You tried so hard,
but the directions
blew away, and
in impatience,
so did I.

LEFT AHEAD

You spoke of
alien invasions,
and listening,
I understood
how you woke up
sad and slept
in anguish,
one foot across
the sea on clay cliffs
ancient buried
and left,
the other beneath you
in fields of rice
and stale water.

Your words were
split over the world.

I was not surprised
when I found your
account deleted
one morning,
all traces of the clay
you once molded
gone, the choice
for field and feet
more stable
than the past
built on drive-throughs
and early sales.

I don't blame you
for choosing,
but I dream sometimes
of eating bowls and bowls
of rice in your old apartment
while a soft voice
sings a requiem
in the background.

HERMITAGE MUSINGS

The winter before
he'd tried to love,
but finding little
solace in it,
opted for the quiet
of sardine cans
and twenty flavors
of ice cream.

He thought of loss
only when he scraped
the bottom of the carton
with the metal spoon
he'd found beneath
his pillow one morning
after sleeping in.

Eventually he only
thought of survival,
and how he
needed more wood
to burn.

He forgot how
to be human
in the early spring.

FROM THE SMALLEST MOUTH

The pepper rolled
on its side until
it hit the water pitcher
and stopped.

No one spoke.
We all waited
for the next words.

The potato salad
bowl was empty,
and when he stood,
Mama picked it up
and returned her
portion to it.

A mosquito buzzed
around my head,
wings whirring in
an annoying whine
until he finally said
that a child can have
too many daddies.

No one passed
dessert.

ODE TO THE REJECTED

Fifty hands came
to the rescue
and counting,
I watched the
shadows work
around my limbs.

Frightened,
I tried to push
flesh away from
flesh, but it
melded into
tree trunks
sprouting from
my torso.

When they left,
I was in pieces
but my mind
was still agile.

I could not
help but wonder
what the rejected
tissue looked like
alone in the
trash receptacle,
swaddled in
green plastic.

FLOW DIVERTED ERROR

Speech was different
then, words bubbling
from lip to cheek,
and the birds
flew South without me.

The ice storm was
significant that year,
and the trees fell
without hope
of remaining upright.

I welcomed the snow
when it blew in,
how it felt melting
against my fevered flesh,
but didn't try speech
again until Spring.

The seasons didn't
last long enough,
and before I could
find the right syllables,
the birds returned.

When they departed,
I went with them.

REVELATION PLATES

Over panini and rye,
I realized you were
not the person
I thought you would be,
and worse,
neither was I.

Katarina Boudreaux is a New Orleans writer, musician, composer, tango dancer, and teacher—a shaper of word, sound and mind. She is the founder of K. and the Ra-Ra Racket, a New Orleans traditional band, and Orquesta Fleur, a tango orchestra based in New Orleans. She manages Dance Quarter, a dance school for all ages which provides lessons in partner dancing from Bachata to Waltz.

Her play *Awake at 4:30* was a finalist in the 2016 Tennessee Williams Festival. Her novel *Still Tides* was a semi-finalist in the 2016 Faulkner-Wisdom competition. Her first novel *Platform: Dwellers* is forthcoming from Owl Hollow Press. Future publications include works with Snow Leopard Publishing and Thurston Howl Publications. *Anatomy Lessons* is available from Flutter Press. www.katarinaboudreaux.com